CONTENTS

INTRODUCTION

WHAT ARE TANGLE STITCHES?

TANGLE ART is drawing repetitive patterns within simple structures. With a little instruction and practice, anyone can learn to draw and create the simple beauty that is a tangle drawing. We have probably all seen variations of this type of drawing and have more than likely sat through meetings or classes aimlessly doodling while we listened to someone speak. This book will show you how to draw with purpose and intention, creating repetitive patterns within a specific area of space with the goal of creating art.

Being able to draw these repetitive patterns over and over again allows our brain to remember the sequence. This makes it easier for us when we stitch those same patterns on fabric. Some tangle patterns are similar to quilting patterns. This is because we take our inspiration from the world around us, and people create what they see. Some of the shapes are very basic and are seen in nature and in historical examples of art and craft. Take a look around your immediate environment and I am sure you can find a pattern or two that could be drawn or quilted.

All patterns used in this book are either official Zentangle patterns or tangle patterns I have created myself. There are many other patterns available on various Internet sites if you do a general search for tangle patterns. The creative and inspirational work that is freely available to view on the Internet is amazing. I hope this book will inspire you as well, not only to create some lovely usable projects but also to experiment and vary the patterns to give them your own twist and personal flair.

> **NOTE:** The Zentangle® art form and method was created by Rick Roberts and Maria Thomas. Zentangle materials and teaching tools are copyrighted. "Zentangle" is a registered trademark of Zentangle, Inc. Learn more at www.zentangle.com.

TOOLS FOR DRAWING AND STITCHING

THERE ARE MANY TOOLS, SUPPLIES, and gadgets that you can use for drawing and stitching. Although we may collect many throughout our creative journey, we only need a few to get started: pen and paper for drawing, and needle, thread, and fabric for stitching. Start with a few items, buying the best quality you can afford. Creating art with good-quality materials is a pleasure in itself.

Drawing Tools

To start drawing tangles, all you will need is a sheet of paper and a pencil. This is enough without having to go and buy special things. If you want a few more tools, you can buy a Zentangle Kit or you can collect your own materials for tangling. Your kit could include:

- acid-free, 100% cotton, heavyweight, fine artists' archival printmaking paper
- fine-point black pens
- soft-leaded pencils to draw your strings and shade your tile
- pencil sharpener
- instructional materials to guide and inspire you

Along with this book, look for others to guide you, including *One Zentangle a Day* (Quarry), *The Art of Zentangle* (Walter Foster), and many others; as well as unlimited instructional materials available online. As you learn to tangle and gain experience, you will also come to appreciate fine-quality papers and tools.

For best results, choose a fine-point pen that uses archival pigments instead of dyes to create a 0.25 mm width line. The ink should dry fast to a neutral pH and be waterproof, chemical resistant, not affected by

A collection of Moleskine Journals

temperature, and permanent on paper. It should also be permanent when heat-set on fabric. Quilters have used these fine-point pens for years to make labels for the back of their quilts. My favorite sizes are 0.25 mm and 0.20 mm in black for drawing on paper. I also use a 0.45 mm size for blocking in large sections. A white gel pen is just perfect for writing on black fabric and paper.

Any soft-leaded pencil will do. The small half-size pencils are handy to pack into a drawing kit to take when you are on the go.

The use of an eraser is controversial within the tangling community. We all know that a "mistake" can be an opportunity to bring another dimension to your drawing. Therefore, there are no mistakes when you are tangling. However, I often like to erase string lines

(continued)

or grid lines on my paper and I use a kneadable putty eraser to soften the graphite shading on drawings. I also use a foam eraser for erasing heavier lines and cleaning up the edges of my work.

You cannot get past using a good-quality heavy-weight paper. I like to use hot press watercolor paper for my art. When designing quilting patterns, I will use whatever paper is on hand, often computer printer paper or a cheap scrapbook. Scrapbooks are great for keeping your notes and drawings organized and are easier to store and refer back to later for inspiration.

One of my favorite ways to keep drawings is to do them directly in a Moleskine journal. I love the water-color notebooks and often use the heavier paper of the watercolor field journals because they are a handy size to tuck into your bag.

Stitching Materials and Tools

Stitching tangle patterns is a lot of fun. It can appear quite intricate and difficult to achieve with a sewing machine; however, if you have a beginner level of skill in free-motion quilting, you will be able to do this successfully. I cannot overstate the benefit of practice. Practice is your best friend, and the more you do, the better your quilting will become. I look back at some of my early quilting days and can see quite clearly how far my work has progressed. It has progressed because of all the practice I do together with a little bit of patience thrown in for good measure.

The pincushion project on page 26 requires only the straight stitching sewing machine foot. The journal cover on page 20 is a hand-stitched project using beautiful felt and silk embroidery threads. Mini Quilts (page 16) require you to use your sewing machine with the free-motion quilting foot.

Sewing Machine

You will need a basic sewing machine that has both a straight stitch and a free-motion foot, (sometimes known as a hopping or embroidery foot). You should be able to drop the feed dogs down or cover them to make free-motion quilting easier. A knee lifter is a bonus, but is not absolutely necessary.

Fabric

Use any good-quality 100 percent cotton quilting fabric when quilting tangles.

Batting

Batting that has a nice loft of about $1/4$ inch (6 mm) is perfect. A wool/polyester blend is nice to use for place mats and table runners because it is easy to launder, and 100 percent cotton is lovely to use for other items such as wall hangings. When making some of the smaller items, you can use scraps of whatever batting you have left over from other projects.

Buttons

Buttons, buttons, and more buttons. You can never have enough, really! I recommend you have some plain buttons for the bottoms of the pincushion project, but look around for something special for the top button. You can find some beautiful glass and vintage buttons in online stores, fabric and quilt stores, or antique shops. Interesting buttons will make your pincushion project a special piece.

Fiberfill

Any good-quality toy filling or stuffing is what you will need for the pincushion project. I like polyester stuffing because it doesn't tend to lump up when you stuff it tight into corners.

505 Spray and Fix

This is a temporary adhesive for fabrics and papers. It is used as a quilt-basting spray to hold layers together because it does not gum up the needle when quilting by hand or machine.

606 Spray and Fix

This spray is used to create a fusible fabric or stabilizer. It is sprayed onto the back of fabric or stabilizer and allowed to dry. The fabric is then placed glue side down against another piece of fabric. An iron set on medium heat is used to activate the dry 606 spray, adhering the glue to the fabric. The hand of the fabric is still quite pliable.

Mistyfuse

This is a paperless fusible web used for fusing two surfaces together. Mistyfuse is lightweight but strong. It is placed between two pieces of fabric and/or stabilizer and is activated with an iron set on medium heat.

Fast2fuse Heavyweight Interfacing

This is a product manufactured by C&T Publishing. It is a double-sided, fusible, stiff interfacing that is easy to mark, cut, and fuse.

Water-Soluble Stabilizer

You can draw patterns directly onto water-soluble stabilizer, stitch your project, and then totally dissolve the stabilizer with water, leaving a beautifully quilted piece of work. In the US, this product is called Solvy, made by Sulky. Victorian Textiles in Australia makes a brand called Aquaweb, which feels like paper toweling and can be temporarily adhered with 606 Spray and Fix.

Freezer Paper

Household freezer paper is useful when you are drawing or writing on fabric. Iron the waxy side of the paper onto the back of the fabric and it will provide a stable surface on which to write. Don't forget to remove the freezer paper when you are finished.

Heat-Erasable Pens

This is one of my preferred ways for marking patterns onto a quilt. There are various brands of iron-off pens available at quilt and craft stores, but be sure to test them before you use them on your final project. They come in a number of colors that all work the same way. This pen can be ironed off quite simply with a dry iron.

Water-Soluble Pens

There are many brands of water-soluble pens available. I highly recommend testing any marking pen you are going to use, preferably on a scrap piece of the same fabric you will be using in your project. Look for pens that have a fine tip and wash out easily. Be mindful that water-soluble pens can become permanent if you iron them. If you are using a water-soluble stabilizer, a water-soluble pen is suitable.

Fabric Markers

These markers are permanent when heat-set on fabric. Make sure you follow the manufacturer's directions. Use these markers when you want a bit of shading or definition on your quilting. The markers come in a range of colors.

(continued)

Needles and thread

Silk embroidery thread

General sewing supplies

Needles

When hand stitching with silk threads or thicker pearl cottons use chenille needles in size 18/24. The eye is large enough to easily thread the larger diameter threads. For hand stitching seams closed, use your favorite hand-sewing needle.

Sewing Thread

The choice of thread is almost endless. For quilting and hand sewing, I prefer 50 weight threads. They are available in a wide variety of colors and thicknesses.

Metallic Thread

My choice is Superior metallic threads. They have a nice range of colors and the thread is flexible enough that I have never had a breakage while stitching with this thread.

Silk Embroidery Thread

For the Hand-Stitched Journal Cover project (page 20), I used hand-dyed silk embroidery threads. I love the feel and sheen of silk thread. It adds that something special to your work.

I have also used DMC No. 8 100 percent cotton perle thread on black and white journal covers to showcase the different effects you can achieve with the same project just by changing the colors. You could also use sashiko thread, which comes in a variety of solid colors. These threads are readily available at all good craft or speciality needlework stores.

Felt

Wool felt is usually made from 100 percent wool fiber felted mechanically to produce a smooth fabric that does not fray. It can be hand dyed in myriad colors. If you are making your own felt from wool top or roving, it will shrink up to 50 percent when wet felted, so remember to make your piece larger than what is required for the finished item. You could also use recycled 100 percent wool sweaters and felt the fabric by washing it first. I urge you to experiment.

General Sewing Supplies

You'll need scissors, pins, a rotary cutter, a transparent ruler, and a self-healing mat.

TRANSFERRING DESIGNS TO FABRIC

THERE ARE A NUMBER of different ways to transfer designs to fabric. Some are as simple as drawing the design directly onto the fabric, others require tracing or using a water-soluble medium, and still others call for printing onto fabric with your computer.

Tracing a Design from a Drawing

Use a light box or window. If you are using your window, it is best to tape the item to be traced directly onto the window so it doesn't move while you are tracing it. If you don't own a light box, a temporary light box can be made by putting a light underneath an acrylic sewing machine table, if you have one, or a sheet of clear plexiglass. My handy husband made me one from a plastic tub, a Perspex (Plexiglas) sheet cut to fit, and a fluorescent light bulb with an on/off switch. It is very robust and durable and provides a large tracing surface. Use iron-off or

HOW TO PREPARE FABRIC FOR PRINTING USING BUBBLE JET SET

MATERIALS
- 100% cotton fabric
- Bubble Jet Set
- freezer paper
- ink-jet printer

1. Soak the fabric in Bubble Jet Set.

2. Remove the fabric from the solution, and allow it to dry. When the fabric sheet is dry, iron a sheet of freezer paper, wax side down, onto the wrong side of the fabric with a dry, warm iron. I am usually impatient and dry the fabric sheet with the iron first.

3. Cut the sheet to the same size as your printer paper (usually 8 ½" × 11" [21.6 × 28 cm]). Remove any loose threads and make sure the freezer paper is adhered to the fabric on all edges. Iron down any loose edges after cutting.

4. Place the fabric/freezer paper sheet into the paper feed tray on your ink-jet printer. Only feed one sheet through the printer paper feed tray at a time. Before printing, set the print quality to grayscale or draft, which should still be dark enough for you to see clearly.

water-soluble pens to transfer the pattern onto your fabric while working at the light box.

Using a Water-Soluble Stabilizer

You can draw directly onto this product with a water-soluble pen, place it on your fabric, and stitch through. It can be thoroughly removed with water.

Printing onto Fabric

If you have an ink-jet printer, you may wish to print directly onto your fabric. Many brands of ink-jet printable fabric sheets are widely available. Check your local craft and fabric stores. Or you can make your own printable fabric using a product called Bubble Jet Set. This is a liquid fabric soak that helps set the ink when printed. Bubble Jet Set is usually available at craft and quilting supply stores. Follow these instructions for preparing fabric for printing with Bubble Jet Set. Like all things, do a test piece first and experiment with it.

5. Remove the freezer paper from the fabric sheet. Iron the fabric sheet after it has been printed, give it a rinse under warm water to remove any loose ink, and then iron it again.

> **TIP:** *I have an old HP printer that I use specifically for printing on fabric and other mediums. I recommend you check your printer manufacturer's guidelines before using it to print on fabric.*

> **TIP:** *You can use a photocopier to enlarge the design to the size desired. The simplest way to do this is by working out the size you want your design to be and dividing that by the size of the design you have printed. Take the resulting answer and multiply that by 100. This equals the percentage you should enlarge or reduce the design by on a photocopier. For example, say your design is 5" (12.5 cm) wide and you want it to fit a space that is 12" (30.5 cm) wide.. The calculation is this:*

$$12 \div 5 = 2.4$$
$$2.4 \times 100 = 240\%$$

> *This means you need to enlarge your design by 240% on a photocopier.*

HOW TO DRAW WITH TANGLE PATTERNS

Hand-drawn tangled tiles

You do not need any drawing experience whatsoever to create beautiful tangle patterns . . . really! It truly is simply a matter of drawing a shape and repeating that pattern and then adding more. Come on, I'll show you how!

MATERIALS

• piece of paper measuring 3½" × 3½" (8.9 × 8.9 cm)

• pencil

• black ink pen

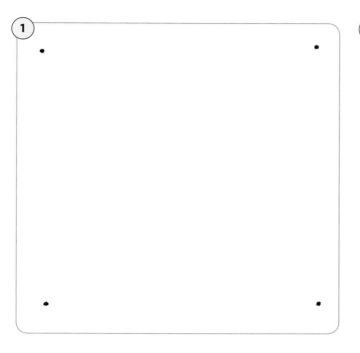

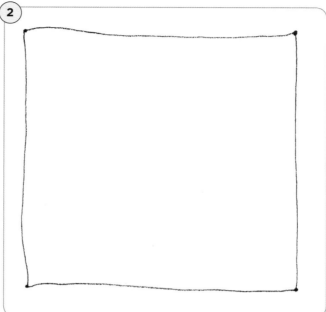

INSTRUCTIONS

1. Start with dots. Using the pencil, place a small dot in each corner of the tile, approximately ¼" (6 mm) in from the edge.

2. Connect the four dots to create a border to frame your drawing. This is also a good way to take away blank paper nerves.

3. Create sections with string lines. A string line is a pencil line that separates the paper into sections where you will draw different patterns. Start with a simple string line. Let's begin tangling with this string line.

(continued)

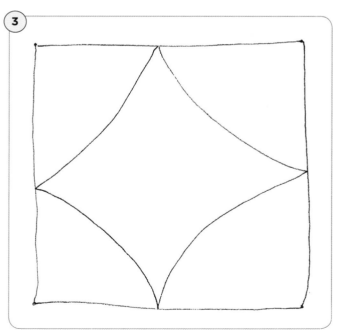

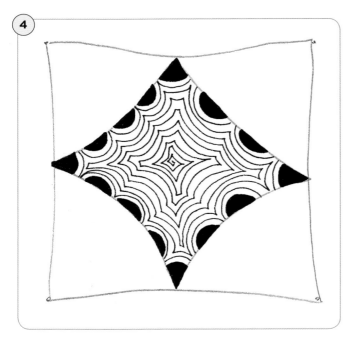

Now let's tangle. Switch to the pen. Within the spaces created by string lines we add the magic of tangle patterns. Each tangle pattern has so many possibilities, so many ways to vary the pattern and make it unique. Refer to the Tangle Patterns on pages 14 and 15 to see the individual pattern instructions, and draw along with me as I add more tangles to the tile.

4. Start with Crescent Moon in the center shape.

5. Add Rick's Paradox to the upper left corner.

6. Next add Msst to the upper right corner.

7. Add Chartz to the lower right corner.

8. Finish the drawing with Echoism in the lower left corner.

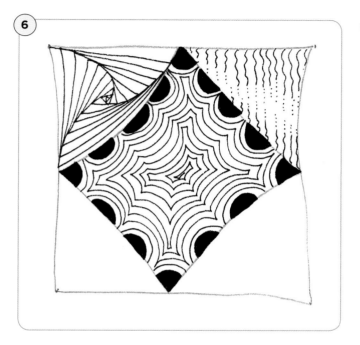

And there you are . . . a small finished piece of art with five different tangle patterns. The variations of strings and patterns are virtually endless, allowing hours and hours of wondrous drawing. You can find more string lines and tangles on my dedicated blog called One Tangle, www.onetangle.blogspot.com, where I post a new tangled tile almost daily.

TANGLE PATTERNS

I HAVE CHOSEN several patterns to show you how to draw them. The pattern directions are commonly known as "step outs." They show you how to create each individual step to make the whole pattern. These five patterns are official Zentangle patterns, and this means they were created and released by Zentangle. I have created and named many other patterns for my drawing and quilting art. Once you get started you will discover ways to change patterns to suit your style of drawing and add your touch, or even create your own unique patterns.

Although most tangle patterns can be stitched, many would require multiple stops and starts. I have included a mixture of patterns, both simple and more complex. Some of the patterns have a more fluid design that will need only minimal stopping, starting, and backtracking while being stitched. When stitching, some elements of the individual patterns can be eliminated, such as the dots in the pattern "Msst" or the colored sections in the patterns "Crescent Moon" and "Chartz." You can add these elements in with a black pen, if you wish.

I recommend drawing any pattern on paper a few times before you start stitching. This makes it easier to stitch smoothly with the machine, and your brain will remember the sequence much more readily if you have practiced first. Let's look at those tangle patterns.

Crescent Moon

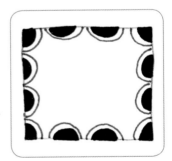  

Rick's Paradox

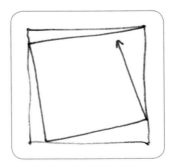 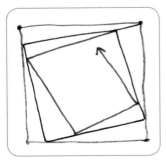 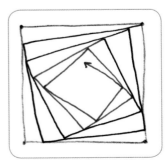 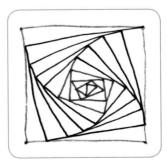

Msst

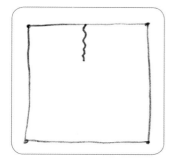   

Chartz

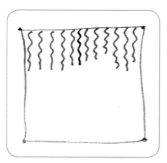 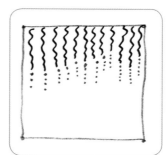  

Echoism

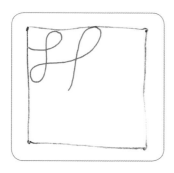 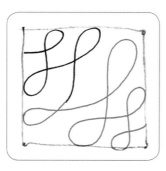  

MINI QUILTS

A mini quilt is a great way to turn your tangle-inspired artwork into beautiful quilted wall hangings or placemats or even pillow fronts. These miniature quilted works of art can be finished off with traditional binding or faced to conceal the stitching from the back. Quilt a set of white placemats with white thread for a subtle yet effective look, or stitch a mini quilt with gold or silver thread for a bit of spark. For a collage effect, quilt several of your tangle drawings in a larger tile, as in the example at right.

The finished piece shown is 12″ × 12″ (30.5 × 30.5 cm); however, you can make mini quilts any size you wish.

MATERIALS

- two 16″ × 16″ (40.6 × 40.6 cm) pieces of cotton fabric
- 16″ × 16″ (40.6 × 40.6 cm) piece of batting
- chalk-based transfer paper
- thread
- 505 Spray and Fix (optional)
- sewing machine

Tangle drawings combined on an 18″ × 18″ (45.7 × 45.7 cm) mini quilt

INSTRUCTIONS

TRANSFER AND STITCH THE DESIGN

1. Photocopy or trace the pattern onto paper. If you wish to enlarge the image, use the formula on page 9.

2. Transfer the design onto fabric using the transfer paper. Start by tracing the outline border and string line, then trace the patterns. The finished project has bubbles inside the top left segment and the inside of the border pattern. The bubbles have been intentionally left out of the pattern to make it easier to see the quilting lines of the main components.

3. Pin the quilt top and batting together securely or use 505 Spray and Fix. A backing piece is not required because this mini quilt will be finished off with a facing rather than a binding.

4. Using your choice of thread, stitch the string line first. Also stitch a line ¼" (6 mm) away from the outside border line, this stitching line stabilizes the quilt and will also be used as a stitching guide line when attaching the facing. Next, stitch the patterns within the string line sections.

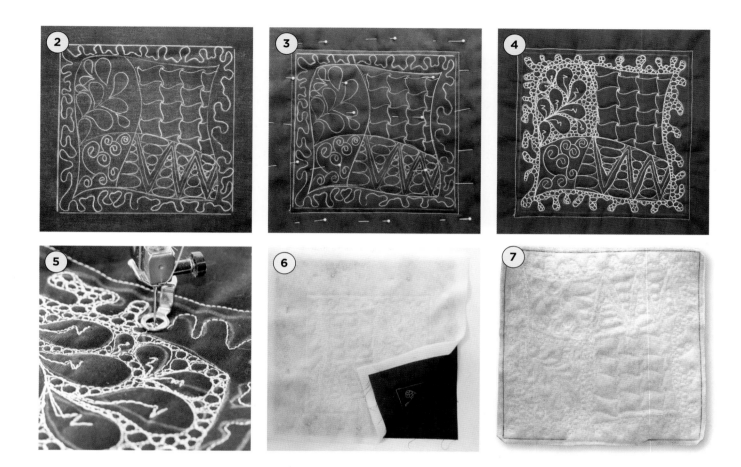

5. Remember to add in the bubbles to the top left section and also to the inside of the border pattern. When stitching the patterns, use the string lines to move between the sections.

ATTACH THE FACING

6. When the quilting is completed, trim each side of the quilt ½" (1.3 cm) from the stitched pattern, leaving a clear margin around the edge. Pin the quilt top and facing fabric with right sides together.

7. To avoid white stitching showing on the black quilt top seams, change the stitching thread color to black. Working from the back of the quilted top, stitch just inside the stitched border line, leaving an opening at one edge for turning. Trim to within ¼" (6 mm) of the stitching line. Trim the corners and turn right side out. Press the mini quilt and hand stitch the opening closed.

HAND-STITCHED JOURNAL COVER

I love journals. I have quite a few and use them to write, sketch, draw, tangle, and paint or stash keepsakes. They are a record of the progression of time, reminding us a little of our history as we go back and look through them. Journal covers can be as outlandish or as conservative as you want. I like neat and tidy stitched edges on my journal covers, with generous inside sleeves so I can tuck bits and pieces into them. This project uses only two embroidery stitches, a straight stitch and a backstitch, which are easily achieved. This design can also be used as a pocket for a bag or as a pillow front.

Finished size 9" × 6½" (23 × 16.5 cm)

MATERIALS

- 9½" × 14" (24 × 35.6 cm) piece of felt
- 9½" × 14" (24 × 35.6 cm) piece of contrasting cotton fabric for the lining
- two 9½" × 9" (24 × 22.9 cm) pieces of contrasting cotton fabric for the sleeves
- chalk-based transfer paper
- ballpoint pen or pencil
- silk and cotton thread for hand stitching
- 6½" × 8½" (16.5 × 21.6 cm) journal or blank visual diary (A5 size)
- rotary cutter, ruler, and mat
- needle for silk thread, such as chenille needle size 18/24
- sewing machine
- point turner

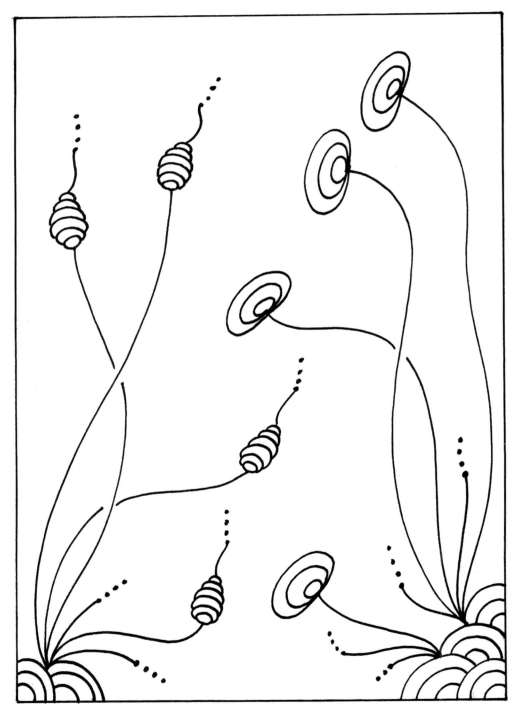

INSTRUCTIONS

MEASURE THE JOURNAL

1. Use this method of measuring and adding allowances for seams to make a fitted cover for any size book, folder, or album. Referring to the photograph, measure the journal from the top to the bottom edge to get the height (H).

2. Measure around the notebook: start from the outside edge of the back cover and go around the spine all the way to the outside edge of the front cover. This is the width (W).

3. Measure the width of the front cover. Add half again of the measurement to get the sleeve width (SW). Remember that the fabric for the sleeve will be folded in half before sewing.

4. Add the seam allowances by following this formula:

Height (H) + 1½″ (3.8 cm)
Width (W) + 1½″ (3.8 cm)

Sleeve width (SW) ÷ 2, then × 3 (or simply take the SW measurement and add half of that measurement)

(continued)

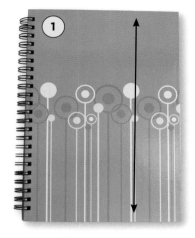

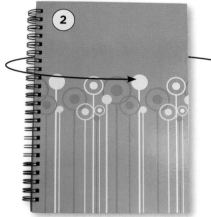

> **TIPS:** *You can use any fabric to make the cover. A quilted name from the previous project would make a wonderful journal cover.*

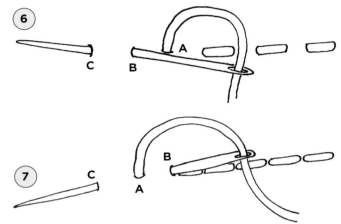

STITCH THE DESIGN ONTO THE FELT COVER

5. Photocopy or trace the design onto paper. Place the design on top of the felt with transfer paper in between. Ensure that the design is ³⁄₈" (1 cm) away from the top, bottom, and side edges. With a ballpoint pen or pencil, trace the design so it is transferred to the felt.

6. Stitch the outside border with a running stitch. Come up at A. Go down at B. Come out at C. Repeat. C becomes A.

7. Stitch the inside design with a backstitch. Come up at A. Go down at B. Come out at C. Repeat. C becomes A.

> **TIP:** If you want to stitch your own design, use a piece of chalk to draw directly onto the felt cover. The chalk will brush off easily with a scrap piece of wool/polyester batting when you are finished.

SEW THE LINING AND SLEEVES

8. If the felt has stretched out of shape during the stitching, place the cover face down on a towel and gently press with a warm iron to get it back into shape. Fold each inside sleeve piece in half with the wrong sides together. Press lightly.

9. Place one sleeve on each end of the lining, making sure the raw edges are aligned with the outside edge and the folded edges face toward the center of the lining. Sew around the outside edge using a ¹⁄₄" (6 mm) seam. This will secure the sleeves in place and also give you a guiding line to stitch around when attaching the front cover.

10. Place the lining face down on the front cover so right sides are together. You will not be able to see the sleeves at this point, which will be turned in toward the center and hidden by the lining. Pin the layers together, and then sew just to the inside of the ¹⁄₄" (6 mm) stitch line on the lining fabric. Leave an opening at the bottom edge, between the two sleeves, for turning. Clip all four corners.

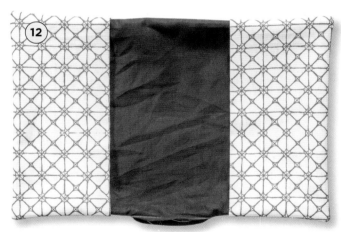

11. Turn the cover right side out. Use the point turner to push the corners out neatly.

12. Iron the cover flat. Place the journal into the cover, and then close the cover to check that the size is not too loose or too tight. Slipstitch the opening closed.

TIP: *If you wish to add beading to your journal cover, do it after it has been constructed; otherwise, you may break a machine needle and ironing will be difficult.*

PINCUSHION
WITH A TWIST

This biscornu is a twisted shaped pincushion, constructed from two squares sewn together on point and stuffed. The word *biscornu* is a French adjective that means "quirky" or "skewed." Nearly all biscornu are worked on even-weave linen or AIDA cloth with counted cross-stitch patterns. It is a design I have always loved, so I developed this delightful quilted version for you to make with fabric.

Finished Size 4" × 4" × 1½" (10.2 × 10.2 × 3.8 cm)

MATERIALS

- two 4½" (11.4 cm) squares of fabric for pincushion top
- two 4½" (11.4 cm) squares of contrasting fabric for the pincushion bottom
- iron-off marking pen
- 4½" (11.4 cm) square of batting
- black and white thread
- needle with matching thread for hand stitching seams
- long needle with strong beading thread to sew buttons
- fiberfill
- 2 buttons, one decorative for the top and one plain to match the cushion bottom
- sewing machine
- point turner for pushing out corners

INSTRUCTIONS

The tangle pattern used in this design is called Rick's Paradox and is stitched with only straight lines. We will be using a square version in this pattern. Here is a quick review.

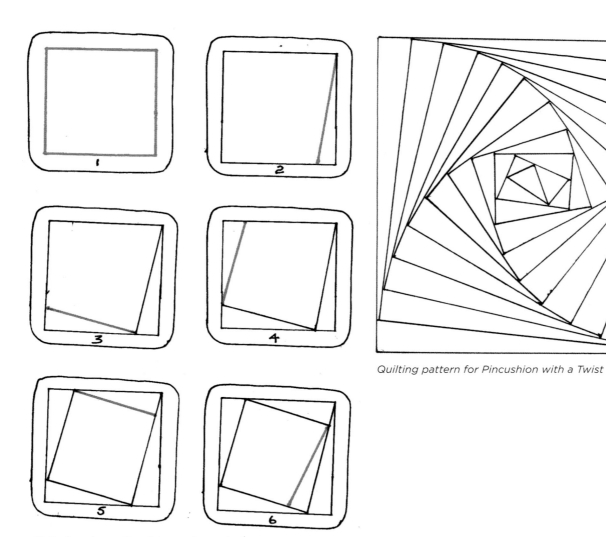

Rick's Paradox pattern step-out

Quilting pattern for Pincushion with a Twist

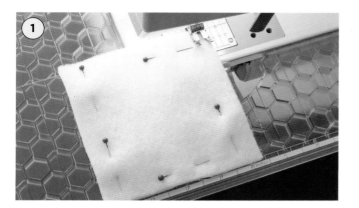

GET THE COMPONENTS READY

1. Place pincushion top fabric squares right sides together and pin the square of batting securely on top.

2. Thread the sewing machine with white thread in the top and bobbin. (I have used black thread in the photos to be seen clearly for demonstration purposes.) Leaving a gap for turning, sew around the square using a 1/4" (6 mm) seam allowance.

3. Clip off all four corners to reduce bulk.

4. Turn the pieces right side out through the opening. Push out the corners with a point turner. Press with a warm iron. Slipstitch the opening closed.

(continued)

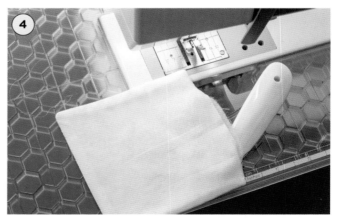

5. Repeat steps 1 to 4 with the contrasting squares, omitting the batting. You now have one pincushion top square with batting inside and one contrasting fabric square without batting. The tangle design will be stitched on the top square, then sewn to the contrasting fabric square to construct the pincushion.

6. Transfer Rick's Paradox design (see page 28) to one side of the top square with the iron-off pen. The outer square should be ¼″ (6 mm) from the edges. Refer to the section on transferring designs to fabric for different methods.

STITCH TANGLE PATTERN

7. Thread your sewing machine with black thread in the top and bobbin. Place the top fabric square under the machine foot and insert the needle in the top right-hand corner ¼″ (6 mm) from the edge. Stitch along the outside square line. At each corner, leave the needle down in the fabric, raise the presser foot, and turn the fabric 90 degrees. Lower the presser foot and continue stitching. When you are back at the starting point, leave the needle down in the work, pivot, and continue sewing the straight lines along the drawn pattern. Pivot at each corner. You will be stitching increasingly smaller lines as you move toward the middle of the square. When you have reached the middle, take a few small stitches to lock your threads. Cut the threads and remove the fabric from the sewing machine. The button will cover this part of the stitching when completed.

TIP: *If you feel confident to stitch this piece without marking, go ahead. It is quite simple once you get the hang of it. As you stitch the first line inside the outer square, aim to end the line just over ¼″ (6 mm) inside the opposite corner. Then pivot 90 degrees each time you reach the previous stitching line until you reach the center of the square.*

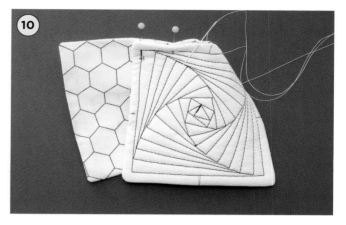

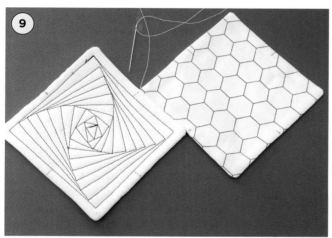

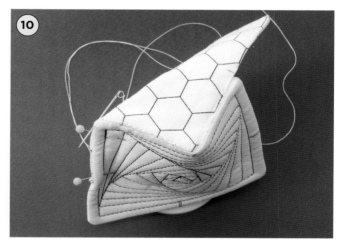

ASSEMBLE THE PINCUSHION

8. Mark the midpoint of each side of each square. Butt a corner of one square to a marked midpoint of the other square.

9. Using a doubled length of sewing thread, slipstitch the two sides together.

10. Continue around the cushion, matching corners to centers, until seven sides have been joined.

(continued)

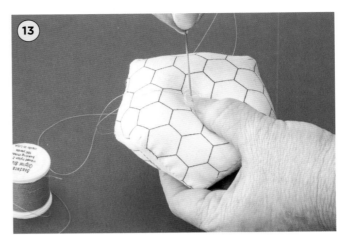

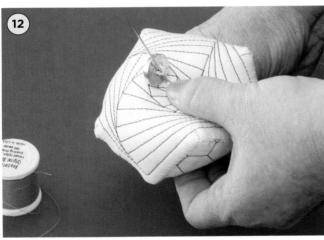

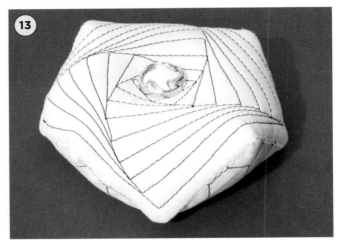

11. Tightly stuff the cushion with fiberfill, and then whipstitch the opening closed.

12. Thread a long needle with a doubled length of strong beading thread. Bring the needle up from the bottom, go through the decorative button shank.

13. Pull the thread back through to the bottom and through the eyes of the plain button. Pull the threads firmly, indenting the pincushion center. Stitch through the cushion and buttons again, and tie off the thread around the bottom button. Clip the threads neatly.